My First Book About Penguins

Amazing Animal Books
Children's Picture Books

By Molly Davidson

Mendon Cottage Books

JD-Biz Publishing

Download Free Books!
http://MendonCottageBooks.com

Read More Amazing Animal Books

Table of Contents

Introduction

Not all penguins are black and white.

Some penguins weigh 100 pounds, others weigh only 2 pounds.

All penguins are unable to fly.

About Penguins

Penguins do not have teeth, their bills just have sharp edges.

Penguins have very large eyes, that can be kept open under the water, so they can see to catch their food.

Penguins ears are on the inside, hidden under the feathers on their heads.

They have very good hearing, and they find their chicks by listeing for their specific sound.

Emperor pengins are the largest, weighing 100 pounds, and standing 3 - 4 feet tall. Fairy penguins are the smallest, weighing only 2 pounds, and standing 16 inches tall.

A penguin has webbed feet, short legs, and a long body, this make them fast swimmers.

When a penguin runs with its wings out to the side, it is usually trying to cool down.

They sleep often, but only for for short periods of time. They sleep laying down or standing up with their head tucked under a wing.

Penguins' Feathers

The layer of feathers closest to the penguin's skin are called downy, and keep them warm.

The next layer of feathers that are over the downy feathers is an oily upper layer of feathers that help waterproof the penguins.

On the penguins' wings they have very short and stiff feathers. These stiff feathers help move the penguin through the water.

Some penguins look blue, because at the tip of each feather there is a blue spot.

Penguins lose all their feathers and grow new ones each year, during this 3 week time they cannot go swimming for food. Their new feathers are not waterproof yet so they would freeze if they did go swimming.

How Penguins Hunt For Food

Penguins have white bellies, which helps camoflauge them. When predators look up to the surface of the water, it looks like light, not food.

Penguins have black heads and backs, this also helps with camoflauge, when they are swiming up to a group of fish, the fish just see dark, like the bottom of the ocean, until the penguins turn over and the fish scatter, making it easier for the pengiuns to catch the fish.

Why Preening is Important

Preening or cleaning their feathers is very important to the penguins.

The penguins need to use their preen gland, that produces oil, for them to cover their feathers in to help them stay waterproof.

The oil also stops bacteria, algae, and dirt build up.

Lastly, it makes them slippery so they can zip through the water.

Caring For Their Young

Penguins lay their eggs in a nest. The mom or dad will stay with the egg to keep it warm under their belly or on top of their feet.

Once the chick is born, it will be warmed by its parents, the same way it was when it was an egg.

Penguins eat fish, but that is too hard for chicks, so the parents will feed their babies fish that has been turned into chewn up porridge.

The King and Emperor penguins lay only one egg while most of the other kinds of penguins lay two eggs.

Chicks cannot see for a few hours after they are born.

Chicks need to stay with their parents for up to a year, before they can survive on their own.

Penguin Groups

There are six groups of penguins.

The Aptenodytes group has the most penguins, and they are also known as the flightless divers. This group has the biggest of all the penguins, and they only lay one egg.

Second is the Pygoscelis, which can also be called the brush-tailed penguins. Their tails have feathers that are very stiff, and can stick out like the bristles on a hairbrush.

Third group is called the Eudyptes. These penguins are known as the crested penguins or beautiful diver. All of the penguins have a golden or yellow crest, which is a group of feathers that goes from their bill around their eyes.

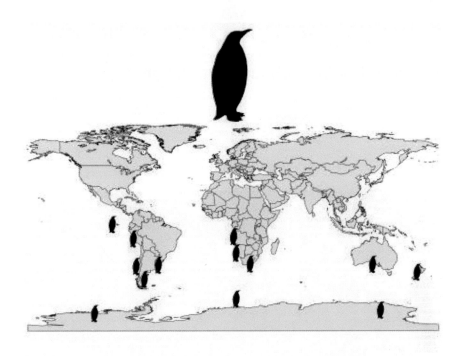

Next is the Spheniscus, also called the banded or wigtailed penguins. All the penguins in this group have a big black band across their chests, and they also have black spots on their fronts.

Fifth is the Megadyptes group, also know as the Yellow-eyed penguin. They are the most rare of all the penguins, they are endangered, and only live on New Zealand's coast.

The final group of penguins is known as the Eudyptula. These are the smallest of all penguins and live in Australia and New Zealand.

Emperor Penguins

The Emperor penguins live in Antarctica.

It is the boy that will hatch the egg, it rests on top of his feet. It takes about 2 months for the egg to hatch.

The Emperor penguin is the largest penguin in the world.

Emperor penguins usually only stay under the water, when hunting, for 2 - 9 minutes.

King Penguin

Their chicks are totoally brown in color.

These penguins are the second largest in size.

King penguins do not waddle, they run really quick instead.

They live in really big groups, called colonies.

Gentoo Penguins

The Gentoo penguins are peaceful, but shy.

They have the biggest tails of all the penguins.

The Gentoos nests are made of rough stones piled in a circle.

They lay two eggs, and both parents take turns keeping the eggs warm and waiting for them to hatch. The chicks will hatch in about 5 weeks.

Gentoo peguins are the fastest swimmers, they can swim as fast as 22 miles per hour (mph)!

Adelie Penguin

The Adelie penguin has a black head and body, with a white ring around each eye.

They lay two eggs, and both parents take turns caring for the eggs on their nest built of stones.

It usually takes about a month for their eggs to hatch.

When the chicks are born, they have gray down feathers.

Chinstrap Penguins

Chinstrap Penguins have a black thin line that stretches out from under their chins.

These penguins have very large colonies that can have as many as one million penguins.

The Chinstrap penguins are known to be the meanest, boldest, and the loudest.

Chinstrap penguins usually hatch two eggs, and their chicks are gray in color.

These penguins prefer to build their nests of stones and on ice-free places.

Rockhopper

The Rockhopper penguin is the smallest species out of all the penguins in the crested group.

These penguins weigh about 6 pounds and stand 19 inches tall.

They like to build their nests in caves, or on slopes and cliffs. This helps to protect them from the harsh weather.

Their nests are shallow and made out of plants and stones.

Erect Crested Penguins

Wikipedia Commons License

The Erect Crested penguins are the only species that can stick their crests straight up to the sky.

They are an endangered species.

Their nests are made out of mud and stones, and their favorite place to build their nests are in caves or along rock cliffs.

Fiordland Penguins

The Fiorland penguins look like the Erect Crested penguins, except their cheeks have white small stripes.

These penguins do not build their nests close to other penguins, and like to build their nests close to the coastline, either in caves or under trees and bushes.

It takes about 4 - 5 weeks for the eggs to hatch, both mom and dad watch the egg.

Macaroni Penguins

Macaroni and Royal penguins look very similar, the only difference is the color of their throats. Macaroni have a black throats, Royal pengiuns have white.

Their nests are simple, and dug out in the soft ground or mud found between rocks.

Royal Penguin

They stand about 23 inches tall, and weigh about 11 to 15 pounds.

Macquarie Island, in between New Zeland and Antactrica, are the only places where the royal penguins live.

Their nests are shallow and dug out from the sand, or between grassy areas with stones or twigs placed around the nest to build it up.

Snares Penguins

Their yellow crests begin at their bill, then wrap around, over their eyes.

Snares Islands, south of New Zealand, is the only place where the Snares penguins breed.

Their nests are made from stones and dirt.

Snares penguins have sometimes been seen resting on a tree limbs.

Humboldt Penguins

These penguins have a black band that runs along their chest area, and they have their own unique black spots.

Chili and Peru are where they breed.

The Humboldt penguins also have flippers that are long, heavy, and they have bare skin just below their bill.

These penguins stand at about 23 inches tall, and weigh about 6 – 11 pounds.

They try to protect themselves from the sun and look to build their nests under bushes or rocks. It will take about 6 weeks for their eggs to hatch.

African Penguins

The African and the Humboldt penguins look very much alike. The African penguin has a shorter tail and their feet are black and pink in color.

Oil spills are a danger to these penguins.

These penguins breed in South Africa along the coast, and on nearby islands.

Magellanic Penguins

The Magellanic penguins are named after the explorer Ferdinand Magellan, who in 1519 sailed around the world.

Magellanic penguins can be found on the coasts of Argentina and Chili in South America.

These penguins are very good at hiding their nests. In fact they are so good that you could be standing right in the middle of one of their colonies and not even realize it!

Galápagos Penguins

The Galapagos penguins live near the equator and have a bare patch of skin under their bill to help them to cool off.

They are shy penguins.

Their homes are burrows they made in the sand or in caves that can be found between old rocks of lava.

Yellow-eyed Penguins

This penguin got its name because their eyes are literally yellow!

They live for about 23 years.

The Yellow-eyed penguins live on Stewart Island, and South Island in New Zealand.

They choose to make their nests between grass and in between bushes. These penguins use plants, grass, and twigs to help build their home.

They lay two eggs, and both eggs usually hatch.

It takes about 6 - 7 weeks for their eggs to hatch.

Fairy Penguin

The Little penguin is the smallest penguin of all the penguins.

These penguins stand about 11 - 15 inches tall, and weigh about 2 lbs.

They live on the coast of Australia and Tasmania.

Once the eggs hatch, the chicks eat at night.

Fun Facts About Penguins

It is called tobogganing when penguins slide over the snow and ice on their stomachs.

The word "crèche" refers to a group of young chicks.

A Penguin's nesting areas are referred to as "rookeries".

A "raft" is when there are many penguins together in the water.

A "waddle" refers to a group of penguins that are together on land.

Most penguins live about 15 - 20 years.

Penguins can see better underwater better than on land.

Penguins must come out of the water every 10 – 15 minutes, to take a breath since they can't breathe underwater.

Penguins swim about 5 – 6 miles per hour (mph), up to 15 mph, just for a burst.

Their average speed for walking is between 1 and 2 mph.

They spend 75% of their lives in the water.

One large penguin can gather up as many as 30 fish during one dive!

Read More Amazing Animal Books

Purchase at Amazon.com

Our books are available at

1. Amazon.com
2. Barnes and Noble
3. Itunes
4. Kobo
5. Smashwords
6. Google Play Books

Download Free Books!
http://MendonCottageBooks.com

Publisher

JD-Biz Corp

P O Box 374

Mendon, Utah 84325

http://www.jd-biz.com/

Mendon Cottage Books

P O Box 374, Mendon Utah 84325

Mendon Cottage Books

17927229R00036

Printed in Great Britain
by Amazon